Network Access

Sys Admin
Reference Reprint Series — Volume 1

R&D Publications
Lawrence, Kansas 66046

R&D Publications, Inc.
1601 West 23rd Street, Suite 200
Lawrence, Kansas 66046-2700
USA

Designations used by companies to distinguish their products are often claimed as trademarks. In all instances where R&D is aware of a trademark claim, the product name appears in initial capital letters, in all capital letters, or in accordance with the vendor's capitalization preference. Readers should contact the appropriate companies for more complete information on trademarks and trademark registrations. All trademarks and registered trademarks in this book are the property of their respective holders.

Copyright © 1994 by R&D Publications, Inc. All rights reserved. Printed in the United States of America. No part of this publication may be reproduced or distributed in any form or by any means, or stored in a database or retrieval system, without the prior written permission of the publisher; with the exception that the program listings may be entered, stored, and executed in a computer system, but they may not be reproduced for publication.

The programs in this book are presented for instructional value. The programs have been carefully tested, but are not guaranteed for any particular purpose. The publisher does not offer any warranties and does not guarantee the accuracy, adequacy, or completeness of any information herein and is not responsible for any errors or omissions. The publisher assumes no liability for damages resulting from the use of the information in this book or for any infringement of the intellectual property rights of third parties which would result from the use of this information.

ISBN 0-923667-50-4

Cover Design: T. Watson Bogaard

The Reference Reprint Series

Sys Admin Magazine flourishes because UNIX system administrators are hungry for serious, technical advice. An article in *Sys Admin* is more than a statement of the problem. It is a complete solution, a battle story from a working administrator who has discovered something useful and wants to pass the word around: tips, tricks, forays into uncharted directories, whole programs with ready-to-use source code. Any article could be the one that saves you from some future calamity.

You never know when a particular *Sys Admin* article will be useful, but the chances are when you need it you'll be thinking about a topic and not about a magazine date, so we designed the Reference Reprint series to serve as a permanent desktop reference with our best advice for UNIX administrators. Here are our most-requested stories, conveniently arranged by subject so you can view the whole set at a glance. If you're a *Sys Admin* reader, here is that one crucial article you might have missed. If you're new to *Sys Admin*, here is the best of what's come before.

And stay tuned for more from *Sys Admin*, the world-wide repository of shoptalk for the keepers of UNIX systems.

To subscribe to *Sys Admin* or order the other books
in the Reference Reprint series, contact us at:

Sys Admin
1601 W. 23rd St. Suite 200
Lawrence, KS 66046-2700
phone: 913-841-1631
fax: 913-841-2624
e-mail: sasub@rdpub.com

Chapter 1

Configuring ftp

Arthur Messenger

Introduction

The current version of the File Transfer Protocol (FTP) is defined in RFC 959, October 1985. Its purpose is to reliably transfer files between computing systems independent of the operating and storage systems.

FTP uses a client-server model. The server side is implemented by a daemon called *ftpd* or *in.ftpd*. The client side is implemented with a program called *ftp*. Figure 1.1 shows a simplified model of FTP.

The client starts the session by opening a control connection with the server, sending the request to port 21/tcp. The client sends its port number, and network address in the connection request. If *ftp* is not available at the network address, the transport provider returns a "connection refused" message. If the request for a control connection is accepted, the *ftp* server sends back a reply code 220, saying that the server is ready, start the authentication process.

The reply code is a three-character digit code followed by a text string. The text string is for human use and is not fixed by the protocol. The digit code is used by the client process and is fixed by the FTP protocol. The first digit tells whether the reply is positive or negative. The second digit tells the reply's category. The third digit, if not 0, is a gradation of the reply. See Figure 1.2 for the meanings of the first two digits.

Once authentication is done and a confirming reply is returned, the client issues commands, and the server responds with replies on the control connection. RFC 959 contains a list of all client commands and server replies. I found that only a subset of the commands available under the FTP protocol are implemented.

If there is data to transfer, the server opens and manages a new connection to transfer the data. It uses port 20/tcp on its side of the connection. By default the client's control port and network address form the other half of the connection. The client can specify another port and network address by using the *PORT* command.

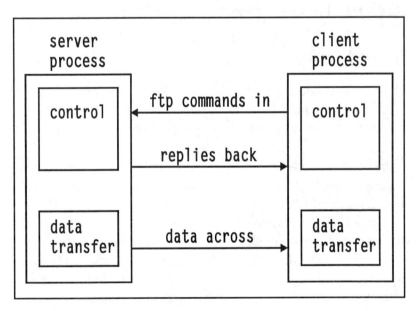

Figure 1.1 *Simplified model of* ftp.

This paper reports on an exploration of the server side of the FTP protocol. I used three versions of UNIX: System V/386 v3.2 from Interactive (SVR3), System V v4.0 from Dell (SVR4), and Sun v4.1.3 from Sun Microsystem (SunOS).

Starting ftpd

On all three operating systems, *ftpd* does not listen for session requests. Instead *inetd* is configured to listen for requests. *inetd* executes *ftpd* once for each request received. If *inetd* is not listening for requests, when an *ftp* request comes in, the client receives a "connection refused" message from the transport provider.

I tried to run *ftpd* as a stand-alone program, mostly to see what would happen because the program is designed to work under *inetd*. I removed *ftpd* from *inetd.conf*. I logged in as root and

```
First digit:

1 Positive Preliminary: more to come, do not send command
2 Positive Completion: done, send next command
3 Positive Intermediate: request for more data, send
                        command completing request
4 Transient Negative Completion: command not accepted, try
                                 again at beginning of
                                 command sequence
5 Permanent Negative Completion: command not accepted, do
                                 not try exact same command
                                 again

Second digit:

0 Syntax: syntax error; command not implemented; message
          not fitting in other categories
1 Information: status or help data
2 Connections: control and data connection
3 Authentication: login
4 not specified
5 File system: status of server file system for a given request
```

Figure 1.2   *Meanings of digits 1 and of reply codes.*

started the *ftpd* program. In each case the program stopped executing with an error message showing there was a problem with its access to the network.

Options of ftpd

The last field of *inetd.conf* mimics starting the program from the command line. This allows the specification of options for the program. *ftpd* has three options:

- -*t*, user inactivity time out;
- -*l*, logging users to *syslog*; and
- -*d*, logging debugging information to *syslog*.

The -*t* option identifies the number of seconds of inactivity allowed before *ftpd* closes the session. Figure 1.3 shows the results of setting the -*t* option to 20 seconds on SVR4. The 421 time out reply code does not show on the screen until another command is issued. The default inactivity time is 900 seconds (15 minutes). The other systems' *ftpd*s acted similarly.

```
$ ftp
ftp > open localhost
Connected to localhost.
220 host FTP server (UNIX(r) System V Release 4.0) ready.
Name (localhost:dianne):
331 Password required for dianne.
Password:
230 User dianne logged in.

<WAITED 20 SECONDS>

ftp > ls
421 Timeout (20 seconds): closing control connection.
ftp > cdup
Not connected.
ftp >
```

Figure 1.3   *Results of* -t *set at 20 seconds on SVR4.*

The -*T* option of SVR3's *ftp* program allows a user to override the -*t* option by specifying the timeout for this session. This has a maximum of two hours.

ftpd writes three levels of messages to the *syslog* daemon facility. Figure 1.4 shows the levels and the types of messages. The *err* level messages are always written. The *info* level messages are written only if the -*l* option is set. The *debug* level messages are written only if the -*d* option is set. The *syslog.conf* file must be modified to direct messages or they are lost.

While testing for the -*l* options, I found that *ftpd* writes login and logout information in the *wtmp* file. Usually, this information is sufficient. On DELL's SVR4 the *wtmp* records have an error and cannot be read by *who*. Here I do use the -*l* option.

The data available from *ftpd*'s -*d* option is difficult to correlate to the actions of the user of the *ftp* client. The same data available from *ftpd*'s -*d* option is available from the client's *ftp* by using the *verbose* and -*d* option. The sidebar "A Sample *ftp* Session with the -*d* Option" walks you through a session with *verbose* and -*d* enabled.

```
Err and warn
   getpeername failed
   getsockname failed
   signal failed
   setsockopt failed
   ioctl failed
   permission denied

Info
   connection from host at time
   User user timed out after timeout seconds at time

Debug
   command received from server
   lost connection
   reply sent to client
```

Figure 1.4   *Levels of messages sent to* syslogd.

Configuration Files of ftpd

Basic access to *ftpd* requires a user to be listed in the server's */etc/passwd* file and to have a password. Anonymous *ftp* does not require a valid password in */etc/passwd*. The files */etc/ftpusers* and */etc/shells* modify the basic requirements.

The file */etc/ftpusers* is a list of account names, one per line, that may not log into the system through *ftp*. I tried this on all

A Sample ftp Session with the -d Option

By default the *ftp* command on both SVR4 and SunOS systems is in the *verbose* mode, which means that the server's replies are shown. Setting the *-d* option causes all of the data to be available on the screen. The following shows such an *ftp* session:

```
1:  $ ftp -d
2:  ftp> open localhost
3:  Connected to localhost.
4:  220 drama FTP server (UNIX(r) System V Release 4.0) ready.
5:  Name (localhost:dianne):
6:  ---> USER dianne
7:  331 Password required for dianne.
8:  Password:
9:  ---> PASS abc123
10: 230 User dianne logged in.
11: ftp> ls
12: ---> PORT 127,0,0,1,4,26
13: 200 PORT command successful.
14: ---> NLST
15: 150 ASCII data connection for /bin/ls (127.0.0.1,1024) (0 bytes).
16: file1
```

systems, and it is true that you cannot login if your account name is in the file. However, this does not apply to anonymous *ftp*. David A. Curry, in *UNIX System Security* suggests:

> As a minimum, the super-user, *root*, and any other accounts with user id 0, should always be listed in this file. System accounts that do not normally have a human associated with them, such as *bin*, *daemon*, *news*, *sync*, *sys*, and *uucp*, should usually be listed as well. (page 70)

```
17: file2
18: 226 ASCII Transfer complete.
19: 14 bytes received in 0.02 seconds (0.68 Kbytes/s)
20: ftp> quit
21: ---> QUIT
22: 221 Goodbye.
23: $
```

Line 1 is the user request to start an *ftp* session with the *-d*, *debug*, option.

Line 2 is the user command to start a connection to the *ftp* port on the host *localhost*. Line 3 is *ftp* informing the user the connection is made. Line 4 is an echo of the reply code coming from the server. The 220 command tells the client machine to send the next command.

Line 5 is *ftp* requesting the account name to use in the *ftp* session. The material in parenthesis is the default if an *enter* key is pressed. Line 6 shows the *USER* command sent to the server.

Line 7, the 331 reply, is the reply to line 6. The first 3 of the code is a Positive Intermediate response. The second 3 shows that the response concerns authentication. Looking up the 1 code in RFC 959 shows the account name is okay and that a password is required. The text accompanying the reply code indicates this.

For SVR3, the file */etc/shells* determines which additional shells are allowed over the standard shells: */bin/sh, /bin/ksh, /bin/csh, /usr/bin/sh, /usr/bin/ksh, /usr/bin/csh*.

The SVR4 */etc/shells* file works slightly differently. If the file does not exist, then only the standard shells *sh, ksh,* and *csh* in */bin* and */usr/bin* are allowed to login using *ftp*. If there is an */etc/shells* file, then only accounts with a listed shell can use *ftp*. If the file is empty, then no one can use *ftp*.

Line 8 is *ftp* asking the user for the password. Line 9 shows that the password is sent across the network in clear text. Since *ftp* is designed to be operating system-independent, the easiest thing to do is to send the password to the server and let it do the authentication. Line 10 is the reply to the *PASS* command of line 9.

Line 11 is an *ls* command issued by the user. If the *ftp* program does not want the data coming back on its control port, it issues a *PORT* command, line 12. Line 13, reply code 200, shows the server was able to set up a new port for sending data. If the port cannot be set up in 60 seconds, the server times out the connection and returns a reply code 425, "Can't open data connection," to the client. This reply code implies that the command can be re-issued exactly as it was given. The 150 reply code of line 15 means that the data is ready to be transferred on the data connection. The ASCII string shows the command used to obtain the data from the file system. Lines 16 and 17 show the data being transferred. The 226 reply code of line 18 shows all data is transferred and the data connection is closed. Line 19 is from the client *ftp* program showing how much data was received from the server.

Line 20 is the user issuing a quit command to the *ftp* program. Line 21 shows the *QUIT* command being transferred to the server. Line 22 is the reply code 221 showing the server is closing the control connection.

SunOS's */etc/shells* file works similarly to the SVR4's except that it uses a different list of default shells: *sh* and *csh* in the directories */bin* and */usr/bin*.

As a result of exploring the options and setup files for *ftpd*, I do the following when setting up *ftpd*: First, I use the timeout option (`-t`) with a value of 300 seconds — five minutes is a long time for no activity. Second, I follow David Curry's recommendations on */etc/ftpusers* and place all super-user accounts and all accounts not associated with an individual in the */etc/ftpusers*. Third, I list all of the shells being used on the system in */etc/shells*. I do not use the option `-d`. I only use the `-l` option on DELL's SVR4.

Configuring an Anonymous ftp

If the system administrator establishes an account named "*ftp*," *ftpd* will allow access to anyone who can *ping* the system using the account name "*ftp*" or "anonymous." Any set of characters works as the answer to the password question; just pressing the enter key does not work. This access method is generally referred to as "anonymous *ftp*."

Each version of UNIX has a set of directions for setting up anonymous *ftp*. The emphasis here is on why the *ftp* account structure must have certain directories and files, and on the tools available to find the necessary directories and files.

The first step is to make sure your *ftpd* does not have known bugs. This means having the current version of the software. I found that the only sure way to know what version of *ftpd* is being used is to talk with the vendor.

In *UNIX System Security*, Curry talks about problems with versions of *ftpd* earlier than July 1989. Node *agate.berkeley.edu* in file */pub/NetBSD/NetBSD-current/src/libexec/ftpd/ftpd.c* shows the current version to be 5.4 (Berkeley) 7/2/91. CERT advisory CA-93:06 shows the current version from *wuarchive.wustl.edu* to be 8 April 1993. Versions of *ftpd* based on the BSD software are probably safe if the version date is later than July 1989. The *wuarchive* version date should be after 8 April 1993.

The second step is to create an account for the anonymous *ftp*. The structure, ownership, and permissions of the account are determined by three conditions. First, the account name must be *ftp*. Second, *ftpd* does *chroot* after accepting the password for the *ftp* account. Third, placement of the home directory is determined by the use of the account.

An entry in */etc/passwd* creates a new account. Figure 1.5 gives a summary of what is in the seven fields. The account name must be *ftp*. Since *ftpd* does not use the password entry, I usually keep it locked. The *uid* is any available user id. The group can be a default user's group. In the *gcos* field we place the words, "Anonymous *ftp* login." The location of the home directory can be any directory (placement of the directory is discussed in the section on downloading and uploading). The initial command field (shell) is not used, but I have seen the *ftp* program placed there. I tried */dev/null* and it worked just fine. I normally place a non-executing file here, */noshell*.

The standard startup files are not necessary for this user. To handle mail that might come to this account, I add an entry to the *aliases* file, forwarding it to another user.

The *chroot* command accepts a pathname as its only parameter. It changes the root directory (*/*), to this pathname. Only a *uid* 0 account can execute this command. (Note: for *chroot(2)* to be effective, the program must then do a *chdir(2)* to */*. Otherwise, . will access the current local directory.)

After executing *chroot*, the kernel does not allow access to any file outside of the local hierarchy, does not allow a *cd* outside of the local hierarchy, and does not allow symbolic links outside of the local hierarchy. Thus, a limited file system hierarchy must be built under the *ftp* account's home directory, the new */*, to contain the files *ftpd* needs. The *chroot* command is executed as part of accepting the password. *chroot* restrictions are in force when the

230 reply code (230 "Guest login ok, access restrictions apply.") is displayed.

The *ftpd* needs access to the *ls* command after the *chroot* to comply with the *ftp* protocol commands *LIST* and *NLIST*. The *ls* command is usually stored under */bin* and */usr/bin*. On all systems I looked at, the 150 reply code to an *ftp dir* or *ftp ls* command shows the path to the command being executed by *ftpd*. The reply shows *ftpd* using the *ls* in */bin*. The limited hierarchy needs the directory *~ftp/bin* to hold a copy of the *ls* command. The permissions on the command should be 111 since *ftpd* needs only to execute the command.

The *ls* command depends on accessing dynamic libraries for some of its subroutines. In SVR4 and SunOS, the command *ldd* lists the dynamic libraries used by a command. SVR3 does not have the *ldd* command; the command *dump* with the *-Lv* options gives the same information. The *dump* command is also available on SVR4. Figure 1.6 shows the results on the different systems. The libraries are stored in */usr/lib* on SVR4 and SunOS. On these systems, the *ftp* account needs the directory *~ftp/usr/lib* with copies of the libraries. On SVR3 the library directory is */shlib*. Here the *ftp* account needs the directory *~ftp/shlib* and a copy of the library. All of the *ls* accessed libraries are needed since *ls* is accessed after the *chroot*. The libraries need the same protection as in the normal hierarchy, so permissions are 555.

account name:	ftp
password:	locked
uid:	any unused user id
gid:	any group id
gcos field:	string "Anonymous ftp login"
home directory:	depends
shell:	depends

Figure 1.5   *Summary of fields for* ftp *account.*

The command *lld* or *dump* must be run on the *ftpd* command since *ftpd* may access libraries after the *chroot*. Figure 1.6 shows the results on the different systems. I tested each library to see if it was needed. SVR3 is easy since both *ftpd* and *ls* need the same libraries. SVR4 shows that *ftpd* needs two additional libraries besides the one needed by *ls*. Experimentation shows neither library is needed. Under SunOS, a quick experiment accessing anonymous *ftp* without the library and with the library shows *ftpd* needs the */usr/lib/libdl.so.1.0* and */usr/lib/libc.so.1.8*

```
SunOS
    $ ldd /bin/ls
        -lc.1 => /usr/lib/libc.so.1.8
        -ldl.1 => /usr/lib/libdl.so.1.0
    $ ldd /usr/etc/in.ftpd
        -lc.1 => /usr/lib/libc.so.1.8
        -ldl.1 => /usr/lib/libdl.so.1.0


SVR4
    $ ldd /bin/ls
    dynamic linker: /bin/ls: file loaded: /usr/lib/libc.so.1

    $ ldd /usr/sbin/in.fptd
    dynamic linker: /usr/sbin/in.ftpd: file loaded: /usr/lib/libnsl.so
    dynamic linker: /usr/sbin/in.ftpd: file loaded: /usr/lib/libsocket.so
    dynamic linker: /usr/sbin/in.ftpd: file loaded: /usr/lib/libc.so.1


SVR3
    $ dump -Lv /etc/ls
            ***TARGET SHARED LIBRARY INFORMATION***
    /bin/ls:
        /shlib/libc_s

    $ dump -Lv /etc/ftpd

            ***TARGET SHARED LIBRARY INFORMATION***
    /etc/ftpd:
        /shlib/libc_s
```

Figure 1.6   *Finding the dynamic library dependencies.*

libraries. SunOS also needs the file */usr/lib/ld.so*, the runtime loader. This file is needed anytime a dynamic library is used. When I leave it out, the error message shows this file is necessary.

For the *ls* command to display the correct information it needs to access the files */etc/passwd* and */etc/group*. Strip these files of all entries that are not needed. The */etc/passwd* file shows only the owners of files and directories. The */etc/group* file shows only those groups associated with files and directories. In fact, the entries can be entirely bogus so long as the *uids* and *gids* match those in the *~ftp* hierarchy. The files are stored in *~ftp/etc*. The files need the same protection they have in the normal hierarchy; permissions are 444.

Commands may access a device file during their execution. On SunOS, the command *trace* shows all system calls and signals for a command given as a parameter. *grep*ing for */dev* shows a superset of the devices needed. On SVR4 the output of the command *truss*, trace system calls and signals, can be *grep*ed for */dev* to find all of the possible device files. On SVR3 neither *trace* nor *truss* exists, so I used *strings*, *grep*ing for */dev*. Figure 1.7 shows that the *ls* command accesses no device files in SVR3. Experimentation shows the only device file necessary in *~ftp/dev* of all those listed by the strings command is *tcp*.

```
$ strings ftpd | grep '/dev'
/dev/null
/dev/log
/dev/console
/dev/udp
/dev/tcp
/dev/ip
$
$ strings ls | grep '/dev'
$
```

Figure 1.7   *Strings of* ftp *and* ls *in SVR3.*

*grep*ing the SVR4 *truss* files for */dev*, as shown in Figure 1.8, and doing some experimentation, shows that *ls* needs */dev/zero* and *ftpd* needs */dev/zero* and */dev/tcp*. The */dev/tcp* is a *STREAMS* device file accessed whenever a *tcp* port is opened. In *STREAMS* on SVR4, multiple transport mechanisms are possible. The file */etc/netconfig* contains information on available transport mechanisms. It is accessed whenever a *STREAMS* device is used to find the underlying transport mechanism. Thus, the file must be available in *~ftp/etc*.

*grep*ping the SunOS *trace* files for */dev*, as in Figure 1.9, shows *ls* needs the device */dev/zero* and *ftpd* needs */dev/zero* and */dev/null*. Experimenting shows the */dev/null* driver is not needed.

```
$ grep '/dev' truss.dev.output
open("/dev/zero", O_RDONLY, 01001077514) = 3
xstat(2, "/dev/ticlts", 0x08047DB4)    = 0
xstat(2, "/dev/ticots", 0x08047DB4)    = 0
xstat(2, "/dev/ticotsord", 0x08047DB4) = 0
xstat(2, "/dev/tcp", 0x08047DB4)       = 0
open("/dev/null", O_WRONLY|O_CREAT|O_TRUNC, 0666) = 2
open("/dev/zero", O_RDONLY, 020000552040) = 3
open("/dev/zero", O_RDONLY, 020000552040) = 3
$

$ grep '/dev' truss.ls.output
open("/dev/zero", O_RDONLY, 01001077024) = 3
$
```

Figure 1.8 grep *of* truss *output files for SVR4.*

```
$ grep '/dev/' trace.ftpd.output
open ("/dev/zero", 0, 07) = 4
open ("/dev/null", 03001, 0666) = 2
$

$ grep '/dev' trace.ls.output
open ("/dev/zero", 0, 07) = 4
$
```

Figure 1.9 grep *of traces from SunOS.*

The device files cannot be copied into ~ftp/dev. The file system entries must be made with the program *mknod*, which makes a special file using the same major and minor numbers for the corresponding device files in /dev. To find the major and minor numbers, do an *ls -l* on the device in /dev. If *ls* is derived from SVR3 or SVR4, then the major and minor numbers are the 5th and 6th fields of the output. If *ls* is derived from a BSD-based system, then the major and minor numbers are the 4th and 5th fields of the output.

Figure 1.10 summarizes the directories, files, and their permissions needed in the ~ftp hierarchy. (Traditionally, there is one

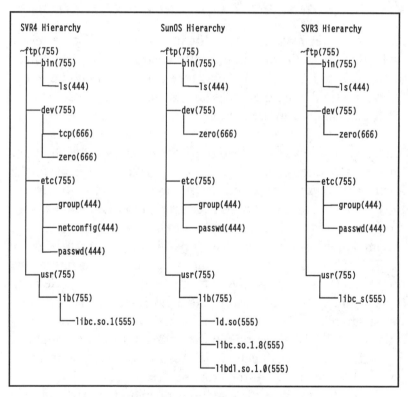

Figure 1.10 *Minimum directories and files needed for anonymous* ftp *in each system tested (permissions).*

more directory. I discuss it in the Uploading and Downloading Directories section.)

One question not decided is who should own the *~ftp* hierarchy. CERT in Anonymous FTP Configuration Guidelines recommends that the *ftp* account's home directory and the subdirectories not be owned by *ftp*. This prevents anyone from making changes to the *~ftp* hierarchy. Without recommending, CERT states that for most systems root is acceptable as the owner of the directories in the hierarchy, and whatever corresponds to root's group is good for the group of the hierarchy directories.

Downloading and Uploading Directories

One more directory, *~ftp/pub*, is traditionally added. If the server will allow only downloading then the permissions on the directory are 755. It's under this directory that you should build the hierarchy used to hold the files clients are allowed to download.

If uploading is allowed, create a directory, *~ftp/incoming*, with the permissions set to 777 to allow anyone to create files in the directory. This opens up *ftp* to some abuses. Placing this directory in its own partition or, if possible, limiting the space available for the directory allows you to protect the system from some of the abuses.

CERT, in Anonymous FTP Configuration Guidelines, suggests a method of hidden directories to limit access to uploading. To implement this, first change the permissions on *~ftp/incoming* to 751. This allows the anonymous *ftp* user to change to the directory but not to list the contents of the directory. Second, create directory names using the same rules as making good password names. Give these subdirectories to *~ftp/incoming* permissions 777. Now anyone knowing a subdirectory name can upload to the known directory. The security of this system is only as good as the password-directory names.

Generally, I follow the directions given in the *ftpd man* page for setting up anonymous *ftp*. I modify the directions to follow CERT's suggestion on ownership of the files and directories.

However, for each system I explored, I found I needed to use `ldd` or `dump -Lv`, and `trace`, `truss`, or `strings` to find missing data.

References

RFC 959. J. Postel and J. Reynolds, October 1985. Available by anonymous `ftp` from host `nic.ddn.mil`, directory `/rfc`, file `rfc959.txt`.

UNIX System Laboratories. *User's Reference Manual/System Administrator's Reference Manual for Intel Processors*. Prentice Hall, 1992. ISBN 0-13-951310-8.

SunOS Reference Manual. Part Number:800-3827-10, Revision A of 27 March 1990.

Anonymous FTP Configuration Guidelines. CERT. Available by anonymous `ftp` from host `cert.org`, directory `/pub/tech_tips`, file `anonymous_ftp`.

Curry, David A. *UNIX System Security*. Addison-Wesley, 1993. ISBN 0-201-56327-4.

Chapter 2

rdist: *A Remote File Distribution Utility*

Judith Ashworth

rdist is a BSD UNIX remote file distribution utility that updates files and directories on remote systems. This utility is quite useful to system administrators for maintaining workstation system files such as root account files which cannot be distributed with NIS (Network Information System — formerly known as Yellow Pages), for installing bug fixes on remote systems, and as a substitute for NIS.

During execution, *rdist* retains the ownership, permissions, and timestamp of the file being transferred. It compares the size and timestamp of the file with the current file on the remote system before doing the transfer, and indicates which workstations were updated. You can also keep the files you want to transfer separate from the corresponding file on the master system by giving *rdist* different source and destination paths.

So how can *rdist* help you? Well, one way is as a substitute for NIS. Suppose you have a number of systems originally set up as stand-alones, and they suddenly need to share the system files usually distributed with NIS. Typically, this would happen when you have the least amount of time to set up an NIS master and get all the client machines on its domain and running *ypbind*. You would probably have to wait until you could schedule some possible downtime to ensure you get it all working.

rdist to the rescue! You can easily transfer a file of any type using this utility — the trick is defining what file you want to transfer, what systems you want to transfer it to, and what you want it called when it gets there.

Using rdist

Fortunately, it's very easy to do once you know how. Before using *rdist*, you would create a file for transfer definitions, which are instructions to *rdist* on what to copy where. In the simplest use of *rdist*, the file would be called *distfile*, and it would be located in the current working directory when you execute *rdist*.

The basic format of a transfer definition in the *distfile* is:

```
<source path> -> <remote host name>
    install <destination path>;
```

where *<source path>* is the full path of the file or directory to transfer, *<remote host name>* is the name of the system to transfer to, and *<destination path>* is what to call it on the remote system.

<source path> may be a list of files in the format:

```
( path1 path2 pathN )
```

Similarly, *<remote host name>* may be a list of host names, using the same format. However, you may not use a list for *<destination path>*.

The *distfile* can be divided up into sections called "packages" that group transfer definitions together so that they may be executed individually by using *rdist* with the package label. Once the *distfile* is created, the *rdist* command is executed by typing:

```
rdist <package name>
```

In cases where you need to keep files synchronized, you can put an entry into the root *crontab* file that will automatically execute *rdist* for you (see the *crontab* man pages, *crontab(1)* and *crontab(5)*, for more information on using *crontab*). If you decide to do this, make sure you use the *-f distfile* option to specify the path of the *distfile* (see the *rdist* man page for a detailed description of this and other options to *rdist*).

Simulating NIS

Here's the solution to our NIS simulation problem. Although in most cases, NIS is the best method for keeping these files up-to-date, you can simulate a portion of what NIS does by using *rdist* to transfer the */etc/passwd, /etc/hosts, /etc/group, /etc/aliases, /etc/auto.master, /etc/auto.home,* and */etc/auto.direct* files yourself.

For the sake of brevity, suppose that only nine systems are affected, and that they are named after Santa's reindeer. Since the files to be transferred are owned by root, the *rdist* command will have to be run as root, and root on the master system must have login privileges on all the workstations involved. This means having the name of the master system in the */.rhosts* file of these workstations.

Caution! Putting the name of any system in the */.rhosts* file allows that system to *rlogin* as root without a password! So putting the name of the master system in the */.rhosts* file is a potential security risk, and you must keep tight security controls on the master system.

For the following examples, I have chosen to create a *distfile* in the */sysadmin* directory on the system called santa. The contents of */sysadmin/distfile* for this problem would look something like Listing 2.1.

What does all this mean? The *nis:* line begins a package definition: it signifies that the following lines can be executed as a group by referring to *nis* on the command line. There can be many packages in the same *distfile*, each separated by a package label, and each can be executed separately. The next five lines indicate the files to transfer and the systems to transfer them to. The last line says to *install* the files on each system at the same destination as the source.

Since it is common for a list of hosts to be reused from package to package, *rdist* has a limited macro facility which allows you to define a macro to represent a list, and then refer to the list by the macro name. The facility is similar to using shell variables. I could have defined a macro called *HOSTS*, and another called *NIS_FILES*, and changed the transfer definition as in Listing 2.2. Using a macro instead of typing a list of files or host names makes the *distfile* easier to read, and the macro can be reused in another package.

Although simulating NIS in this manner may work quite well for a small number of systems, it should not be seen as a long-term solution. It should only be used in the situation where stand-alone systems need to share this information immediately, and then only on a temporary basis until NIS can be set up. A system where NIS is not available would be an exception, and in this case *rdist* would provide a permanent solution.

One of the disadvantages to using this method of distributing system information is that users have to log in to the master system in order to change their passwords for all client systems. In addition, these systems would not get updated with new password information until the next time the */etc/passwd* file is updated, so some sort of automatic transfer or monitoring should be set up.

This method has several other, perhaps undesirable, side effects:

1. Because it replaces the */etc/passwd* file on the client systems, any locally defined entries will be removed. Also, it will change the root entry to be that of the master.

2. It will change the loghost for the clients to the system defined in the /etc/hosts file of the master system.
3. Local mail alias information will be replaced in favor of the master system's definitions.
4. Local group definitions will also be replaced by the master definitions.

Transferring Automounter Mapping Files

Caution should be used when transferring automounter mapping files (/etc/auto.master, /etc/auto.home, and /etc/auto.direct), whether the transfer is being done with *rdist* or NIS. A file system recursion problem will result if a client is also a file server whose exported file system appears in one of the maps. If this is the case, you must provide different maps to NFS servers. This can be done using *rdist* on the master system and specifying different source and destination paths.

For example, assume that rudolf is an NFS server for the /opt file system. The /opt file system contains a bunch of applications, so of course, every workstation needs to access it. As the system administrator for these systems, I want to have the /opt file system automounted, but I don't want it to appear in the *auto.direct* file for rudolf. Also, I want to maintain the *auto.direct* file for rudolf on santa.

rdist to the rescue again! Listing 2.3 shows you how to modify the *distfile* example for this situation. You will see that I removed /etc/auto.direct from the list of *NIS_FILES*, and created a new package called *maps*. I also created a new macro called *MAP_HOSTS*, which does not contain rudolf. The map package has two transfer definitions in it. One transfers /etc/auto.direct to the *MAP_HOSTS*, and the other transfers /sysadmin/auto.direct.rudolf to rudolf, and installs it as /etc/auto.direct.

Now, to get the system files transferred using the *nis* package alone you would type:

```
rdist nis
```

on santa, while in the */sysadmin* directory. If the */etc/passwd* file alone had changed, the screen would look something like this:

```
santa:/sysadmin> 2 # rdist nis
updating host dasher
updating: /etc/passwd
updating host dancer
updating: /etc/passwd :
updating host rudolf
updating: /etc/passwd
```

rdist displays a message for each host, followed by an update message for each file transferred. If a file did not already exist, the message would say "installing" rather than "updating." One advantage of using *rdist* over writing a script for this sort of file tranfer is that the file is not transferred if there have been no changes.

Other Uses for rdist

Another good use for *rdist* is keeping root account files like .*login* and .*cshrc* consistent from system to system. Suppose you are responsible for fifty remote systems and periodically need to *rlogin* to them as root. Remote system administration can be difficult when you have different aliases, environment variables, etc., set up on each system. The root environment can be even more of a problem if workstation owners can change these files. Now you can use *rdist* to ensure that the .*login* and .*cshrc* files remain in sync on every system! Just add the package definition to the *distfile* as shown in Listing 2.4.

Since this use of *rdist* is a good candidate for routine automatic transfer, Listing 2.5 shows an example of a *crontab* entry which would execute the root package every Monday morning at 7:00 A.M.

Here's another example of *rdist*'s capabilities. Suppose you administer a master server that maintains utilities for a large client base, including other master servers on different domains. Making sure that clients have the most up-to-date versions of these utilities while keeping them from NFS mounting across gateways can be quite a hassle.

Since it is capable of maintaining entire directories, *rdist* can easily solve this problem, and, in fact, there is an example in the *rdist* man page. The tough part is defining which servers the clients will be allowed to mount the directory from, and then making sure the master that has the current utilities has root login privileges, as discussed earlier.

Whether you use it to distribute files and directories on an as-needed basis, or to routinely synchronize important system files, *rdist* can be a powerful tool for administering remote systems. The *rdist* utility has several other capabilities that are described in the man page. It can compare a file's timestamp to a timestamp file in order to determine if the file needs to be transferred, save a file as a particular user on the remote machine, notify a specified user about files transferred and errors encountered, and it can even execute a command after each file is transferred. These capabilities are beyond the scope of this article, but now that you know the basics, you are well on your way to understanding the rest!

Listing 2.1 *Simulating NIS example.*

```
# Distfile for rdist command
nis:
        ( /etc/passwd /etc/hosts /etc/group /etc/aliases /etc/auto.master
          /etc/auto.home /etc/auto.direct ) ->
                ( dasher dancer prancer vixen comet cupid donner blitzen rudolf )
                install;
```

Listing 2.2 *Macro example.*

```
# Distfile for rdist command
HOSTS = ( dasher dancer prancer vixen comet
          cupid donner blitzen rudolf )
NIS_FILES = ( /etc/passwd /etc/hosts /etc/group /etc/aliases /etc/auto.master
              /etc/auto.home /etc/auto.direct )
nis:
        ${NIS_FILES} -> ${HOSTS}
                install;
```

Listing 2.3 *Automounter maps example.*

```
# Distfile for rdist command
HOSTS = ( dasher dancer prancer vixen comet cupid donner blitzen rudolf )
NIS_FILES = ( /etc/passwd /etc/hosts /etc/group /etc/aliases /etc/auto.master
              /etc/auto.home )
MAP_HOSTS = ( dasher dancer prancer vixen comet cupid donner blitzen )
nis:
        ${NIS_FILES} -> ${HOSTS}
                install;

maps:
        /etc/auto.direct -> ${MAP_HOSTS}
                install;

        /sysadmin/auto.direct.rudolf -> rudolf
                install /etc/auto.direct;
```

Listing 2.4 — *Root environment example.*

```
# Distfile for rdist command
HOSTS = ( dasher dancer prancer vixen comet cupid donner blitzen rudolf )
NIS_FILES = ( /etc/passwd /etc/hosts /etc/group /etc/aliases /etc/auto.master
            /etc/auto.home )
MAP_HOSTS = ( dasher dancer prancer vixen comet cupid donner blitzen )
nis:
        ${NIS_FILES} -> ${HOSTS}
                install;

maps:
        /etc/auto.direct -> ${MAP_HOSTS}
                install;

        /sysadmin/auto.direct.rudolf -> rudolf
                install /etc/auto.direct;
root:
        (/.login /.cshrc) -> ${HOSTS}
                install;
```

Listing 2.5 — crontab *example.*

```
00 07 * * 1 /usr/ucb/rdist -f /sysadmin/distfile root
```

Chapter 3

Keep Watch with a Sentinel

William Genosa

System administrators are responsible for ensuring the availability of their machines to users. When servers crash or backups fail, the users are inconvenienced, which will most likely result in trouble for the system administrator. If you are a sys admin for more than one machine and your machines are networked together with TCP/IP, then you may want to set up a Sentinel to watch over your network and inform you of a system crash or backup failure. A modem and a beeper would also be required.

My network consists of eight 3B2 hosts running AT&T System V v3.2.2 networked together with TCP/IP over ethernet. The Sentinel is *cpu4* and the two servers I am concerned with are *cpu5* and *cpu8*. My servers reboot each weeknight and run unattended level zero backups to back up the entire system. A failure on a server would result in downtime the next morning that would cost my company thousands of dollars. If a server crashes at night, the Sentinel alerts me so that I can take corrective action before my users arrive in the morning. This makes my boss very happy.

The program makes use of the *ruptime* command, which displays the status of hosts on a local area network. Output of the command uses the following format:

```
cpu1    up       9:40,     5 users,   load 0.04, 0.08, 0.05
cpu2    up    2+04:25,     8 users,   load 0.08, 1.23, 0.40
cpu3    up       8:35,     5 users,   load 1.00, 1.01, 1.06
cpu4    up       8:43,     6 users,   load 1.04, 1.00, 0.95
cpu5    up       8:47,    75 users,   load 4.60, 3.90, 4.65
cpu6    up    5+07:50,     0 users,   load 0.00, 0.00, 0.00
cpu7    down     0:20
cpu8    up       8:45,    65 users,   load 4.70, 4.20, 3.85
```

The first field represents the name of the host. The second field displays the status of the host. The third field shows how long the host has been up and running in days, hours, and minutes. The fourth and fifth fields tell how many users are currently logged in. The last four fields display the system load or average number of processes over the last one, five, and fifteen minutes.

The program also makes use of *uucp*. My backup scripts have been modified to test for the exit status of *cpio* because I use *cpio* to create backups. If the backup is successful on the server, I send a file to *cpu4*, the Sentinel, using the following commands:

```
cpio -Obv -O/dev/RSA/qtape2 < /tmp/backup.list

if [ "$?" -ne 0 ]
then
     echo The backup failed on 'hostname' at 'date'. | mail root
else
     echo The backup was successful on 'hostname' at 'date'. | mail root
     >/tmp/backup.ok
     uuto /tmp/backup.ok cpu4!bill
fi
```

The routine tests for a successful backup by testing the exit status of *cpio*. The *if* conditional checks *$?*, the exit status. If the exit status is zero, I create a zero-length file called *backup.ok* and send it to *cpu4* using the *uuto* utility. If sent from the server *cpu5*, this file would be sent to *cpu4* and be placed in the directory */usr/spool/uucppublic/receive/bill/cpu5*. If the Sentinel doesn't find the file */usr/spool/uucppublic/receive/bill/cpu5/backup.ok*, it will use the *cu* utility to page me on my beeper.

How rc Scripts Work

All *rc* scripts should reside in the directory */etc/init.d*. The scripts should then be linked to a file in */etc/rc2.d* or */etc/rc3.d*, and */etc/rc0.d*. These directories correspond with the run levels 2, 3, and 0. *init()* will read *inittab* and execute the scripts associated with the run level it is about to enter. When executing the *rc* scripts, *init* passes along an argument to the script. The argument will either be "start" or "stop." Therefore, the same script should be written for starting and stopping a process.

Scripts are executed in alphanumeric order. Scripts to be executed while the system is coming up will usually be linked to files in */etc/rc2.d* and will begin with the letter *S* (for "Start") followed by a number and a name related to the operation, such as *inet*, *cron*, or *lp*. Lower numbers will be executed first. Scripts to be executed while the system is going down should be linked to files in */etc/rc0.d* and begin with a *K* (for "Kill"), followed by a number and a name. Once again, lower numbers will be executed first. *S* files and *K* files may be in the same *rc* directories. The *S* files are run when *init* starts the run level; the *K* files in the same directory are run just before *init* kills that run level. *init* then moves on to the next run level, which has its own *S* and *K* files. This is how the system controls the order of events upon boot and shutdown.

The sample entries here have been appended to the *uucp* configuration file, */usr/lib/uucp/Systems*. Similar entries would be required on your Sentinel host. The first field of the *Systems* file usually represents a host name. I have created bogus host names to allow the Sentinel host the ability to dial a beeper number and transmit a code which briefly describes the problem.

The entries that follow are called with *cu*; they are used to notify the system administrator by sending a code on his or her beeper.

```
### The server called cpu5 has crashed.
cpu5down Any ACU 9600 93631448,,,,,5551111

### The server called cpu8 has crashed.
cpu8down Any ACU 9600 93631448,,,,,8881111

### The backup has failed on cpu5.
badback5 Any ACU 9600 93631448,,,,,5552222

### The backup has failed on cpu8.
badback8 Any ACU 9600 93631448,,,,,8882222
```

The next entry is a sample entry for those of you who have a SkyPager Beeper. Notice the use of the pound key and the trailing comma.

```
Any ACU 9600 918007597243,,,,,6182093#,,,,5551111#,
```

The Sentinel program should run constantly to keep watch over the critical hosts. For this reason I start the program from an *rc* script which runs at boot time. (See the sidebar for a brief explanation of how *rc* scripts work.)

The *rc* script I use (see Listing 3.1) is called *sentinel* and is located in the directory */etc/init.d*. It is then linked to */etc/rc2.d/S99sentinel*. No action will be needed upon shutdown. If there were a need to take action, the same file would also be linked to */etc/rc0.d/K99sentinel*.

The Sentinel program (Listing 3.2) can be modified to monitor other critical events on your network. This is an example of pro-active system administration. Systems will crash and backups will fail but you can still attempt to minimize the effect this will have on you user community.

Listing 3.1 rc *script to call the* sentinel *program.*

```
#!/bin/sh
#############################################################
###                   /etc/init.d/sentinel                ###
### This is the rc script used to start the "sentinel" program kept ###
### in "/usr/bill/progs".     Notice the use of "at" to delay the ###
### start of the  program  till after the  machine  is up for a few ###
### minutes.                                              ###
#############################################################

case $1 in
    'start')
        echo /usr/bill/progs/sentinel | at now +5 minutes   ### set delay
        exit 0
        ;;
    'stop')
        exit 0                                        ### no action
        ;;
    *)
        exit 1                                        ### error
        ;;
esac

### End of File ###
```

Listing 3.2   *The* sentinel *program.*

```
###########################################################
###                                                     ###
###                     SENTINEL                        ###
###                        by                           ###
###                  William Genosa                     ###
###                                                     ###
### The  Sentinel  program runs on a stable  machine and monitors other ###
### computers on the same  ethernet network  using the  TCP/IP  ruptime ###
### facility to check for a  system crash.   Uucp is utilized to send a ###
### file from the  server to the machine which is running the  Sentinel ###
### program.    This was accomplished by modifying the backup script on ###
### the server.  Absence of this file on the  "Sentinel"  machine is an ###
### indication of backup failure.    When the program detects either a  ###
### server has crash or a backup has failed,  it will notify the System ###
### Administrator by calling his  beeper.   Different  codes  allow the ###
### System  Administrator  to determine the problem by seeing the  code ###
### on his beeper.   This program requires the machine running Sentinel ###
### to have  a   modem  available for  dialing out,   and for the  System ###
### Administrator to possess a beeper.   The program should be started  ###
### in one of the rc scripts.                                           ###
###########################################################

while true                         ### Begin infinite while loop.
do

###-------------------- Set up a few variables. ------------------------

HOUR=`date +%H`                    ### Extract the current hour.
DAY=`date +%a`                     ### Extract the current  day.

###--------- Test to see if the two main servers are running. -------------

### Cron schedules the two main servers to reboot at 7pm each night. If the
### hour is NOT between  7pm  and  8pm, test to make sure both servers are
### up and running.   One of the servers is called "cpu5" and the other one
### is called "cpu8".
```

Listing 3.2 *continued*

```
if [ ${HOUR} -ne 19 ]
then

     ###--- If cpu5 is down then beep the beeper with code 555-1111. ------

     if ruptime | grep "cpu5" | grep "down" > /dev/null
     then
          cu cpu5down
     fi

     ###--- If cpu8 is down then beep the beeper with code 888-1111. ------

     if ruptime | grep "cpu8" | grep "down" > /dev/null
     then
          cu cpu8down
     fi
fi

###------------- Check to see if the backups completed ok. ----------------

### Cron schedules backups on the main servers every week night. The
### backup scripts test the exit status of cpio used to create the backup.
### If the backup is successful (exit status is 0), then the backup script
### sends the file "backup.ok" to cpu4, the machine where "Sentinel" is
### running. The servers use "uuto" which place the file in the uucppublic
### directory of machine cpu4.  Backups start at 8pm and finish around
### midnight.

### Since Friday nights backup may not complete till Saturday morning, if
### the day is not Sunday, AND if the day is not Monday, AND if the hour is
### 1am, test to see if the backups completed.

if [ ${DAY} != Sun -a ${DAY} != Mon -a ${HOUR} -eq 1 ]
then

     ### If the file backup.ok has not arrived in the uucppublic
     ### directory for cpu5, then the backup probably failed. Beep the
     ### beeper with the code 555-2222.

     if [ ! -f /usr/spool/uucppublic/receive/bill/cpu5/backup.ok ]
     then
          cu badback5
     fi
```

Listing 3.2 *continued*

```
              ### If the file  backup.ok  has not arrived in the uucppublic
              ### directory for  cpu8,  then the  backup probably failed. Beep the
              ### beeper with the code 888-2222.

              if [ ! -f /usr/spool/uucppublic/receive/bill/cpu8/backup.ok ]
              then
                    cu badback8
              fi
       fi

       ###--------- Remove backup.ok files for the next backup. -----------------

       ### If it is 3am and the backup.ok files are present in uucppublic for cpu5
       ### and cpu8,  then we must remove them to prepare for the next backup.

       if [ ${HOUR} -eq 3 ]
       then
              ###------- Remove the backup.ok file for cpu5 if it exists. ----------

              if [ -f /usr/spool/uucppublic/receive/bill/cpu5/backup.ok ]
              then
                    rm -f   /usr/spool/uucppublic/receive/bill/cpu5/backup.ok
              fi

              ###------- Remove the backup.ok file for cpu8 if it exists. ----------

              if [ -f /usr/spool/uucppublic/receive/bill/cpu8/backup.ok ]
              then
                    rm -f   /usr/spool/uucppublic/receive/bill/cpu8/backup.ok
              fi
       fi

       ###---------- Sleep ten minutes before making another check. --------------

       sleep 600

       done

       ### End of File ###
```

Chapter 4

newping: *Remote Host Downtime Detection*

Eric T. Horne

Over the course of nights spent waiting for the Sun cluster in our lab to recover from yet another crash, my lab partners and I reached the conclusion that the main problem with recoveries lay not in the execution but in letting the administrator know that the system was down. In fact, knowing whether a system is down, or even hung, is the first step in solving the problem.

A Tool Called ping

A reasonable tool for this sort of detection might be the *ping(1)* command, which sends an echo request from the source machine to the destination machine. Upon receipt of the echo, the destination machine echoes the data sent along with the echo request back to the source machine. When the source machine receives the echoed data, it reports that the destination machine is up. If the source machine does not get the echoed data within a certain timeout period, the source machine reports the destination as down. *ping* also reports other problems it finds, like unreachable host/network or unknown hostname. Using *ping* in an automated process that checks each host's status is easy to do by incorporating *cron* and script programming. Running the script every X minutes via *cron* is the way to go.

A Closer Look at ping

Looking at *ping* a little more closely, I found that it wasn't as reliable as I had hoped. *ping* uses ICMP (Internet Control Message Protocol) to ask for a simple echo of some data. The data consists of a message number and the time sent from the source. The destination machine receives the ICMP echo request and sends back an ICMP echo reply. When the source machine receives the echo reply, it calculates the difference between the current time and the time data in the reply to find the total elapsed time it took the message to bounce back. If the destination machine is down, the source machine will eventually timeout waiting for a response that will never come.

I didn't really think much about this, in fact I figured it was exactly what I needed, until I stumbled into one important factor. The destination machine CPU never knows about the ICMP echo request, because the Ethernet card handles it automatically. In other words, the Ethernet card intercepts the ICMP echo request and sends the reply all by itself, allowing the CPU to handle other things, like user processes.

Allowing the Ethernet card alone to handle the echo request implies a big assumption on *ping*'s part. *ping* is also misleading the user into thinking that the Ethernet card status represents the machine's status, which is not always true. It is possible that the Ethernet card is responding and handling its ICMP echo requests, while the CPU has come to a grinding halt because of a disk error or some other problem. Like it or not, systems hang, and *ping* won't tell you a thing about it.

A Look at newping

newping's purpose is to help correct *ping*'s shortcomings. While this program performs many of the same services as *ping*, it differs significantly in its function. One significant difference between *newping* and *ping* is the choice of protocols. *ping* uses ICMP, while *newping* uses TCP/IP, which forces itself past the Ethernet card and demands attention from the *inetd*, and thus the CPU, running on the destination machine. The use of TCP/IP allows *newping* to connect() with the destination host via a well-known port. (*newping* uses the TIME/TCP port.) Each well-known port associates itself, thanks to *inetd*, with some sort of daemon, and if not, then with some sort of runnable code. When *inetd* detects a connection to a particular port, it notifies the daemon and redirects the data, if any, to it. The daemon wakes up and handles the request. Notice that the *inetd* and daemon actions both require a response from the CPU, not only the Ethernet card. Both *newping* and *ping* will notify the user of the test results, although *newping* returns much more detailed and meaningful values than *ping*. (See Table 4.1 for some details).

0	Connect and response.
1	Timed out for connection.
2	Timed out for response.
3	Connection refused.
4	Problem with network.
5	Host unreachable.
255	Unexpected error.

Table 4.1   *Return values for* newping.

newping *Code*

Besides the initial startup instructions, the *newping* code is straightforward (see Listing 4.1). *newping* begins by looking at the command line to determine any options and the name of the host to check, also the amount of time, in seconds, to use as a timeout. The program processes all of this information and stores it in several variables and structures used later by *connect()*. After completing verification of other miscellaneous data, *newping* uses *signal()* and *alarm()* calls to set an internal alarm to go off in exactly one second. When the second is up, the alarm calls an action routine, *noconnect()*, which keeps track of the time that has passed. If the time passed is more than the timeout value, a connection was not made within the time limits, and *newping* times out. Otherwise, if the timeout has not been violated, *newping* continues, with the alarm set to go off in another second. In effect, *noconnect()* either gives *newping* another second to connect, or exits *newping* with a return code set to 1 (see Listing 4.2). If a connection is made prior to a timeout, the connection is deemed successful and the next phase begins.

If the connection is successful, which implies that the Ethernet card is OK, *newping* next tests the CPU. A quick call to *signal()* resets the SIGALRM action from calling *noconnect()* to calling *noresponse()*. Both functions perform the same task: the difference between them lies in the status code they return via *exit()* if the count exceeds the timeout value (see Listing 4.3). It is important to notice that the time passed is not reset from the *noconnect()* call. *newping* works in much the same way as the Ethernet card test does. The only real difference is that *newping* calls *recv()* instead of *connect()*. It is simply blocking, waiting for the destination machine to send its data. If *newping* times out before *recv()* detects the presence of any data, the destination machine is most likely a hung machine. The Ethernet card will respond, but the CPU is either so loaded with work it does not have time to return data, or the CPU has halted. Either case is worth investigating.

Recall that *newping* connects to the TIME/TCP port of the destination host. I chose the TIME/TCP port because when it detects a connection, it automatically sends the local time through it and disconnects the connection. The data returned is not used for anything. Its presence means that the machine is responding. Receiving the data allows *newping* to exit with a code of 0. Detecting any sort of error forces *newping* to exit with the proper return code (see Table 4.1).

Automating Detection

newping's ability over *ping* to return distinguishable codes for different states of a destination machine make *newping* very useful for shell scripts. A script using *newping*, a list of destination hosts, and a few loops can be surprisingly effective. Listing 4.4 shows a simple script, worthy of your improvement.

The script in Listing 4.4 acts as a base script. You can change it to match your needs. It could easily be altered to record the times a host went down and came back up again. It could notify a list of people using *write(1)* or *mail(1)* that there is a particular problem with some host. It could even test the stability of a network.

cron can run the script in Listing 4.4 every X minutes, allowing an ongoing, automatic notification system. My department even hooked a terminal to the back of my Sun 4, through */dev/ttya*, to which a script could then write the status of each host in a list. The script in Listing 4.4 can be altered to do this by changing the */dev/console* to */dev/ttya*. We ran our particular version every five minutes through *cron*. This gave us an updated status for every important host in a list with the oldest update only five minutes old. Our script logged host downtime for a monthly report, which summarized how often a system went down and for how long. As your needs change, the script can change with them.

Over time, this simple script grew to be one of the more complicated scripts I have ever written.

newping is not by any means the be-all-end-all method of detecting remote host downtime. Used in the right way, however, it can help to terrifically speed up your response to down hosts.

Listing 4.1 newping.c

```c
/* newping v1.0f

    Replaces ping(1) for simple host status
    information. Uses TCP/IP to check the
    target machine, connects to a well-known
    port, and waits for a response. Does not
    use ICMP, like ping(1).

    Exit Codes:

    0 -- host is up
    1 -- Problem with connecting
    2 -- host would connect, but wouldn't respond
    3 -- Connection was forcably refused
    4 -- Problem with the network
    5 -- Host is unreachable
    255 -- Unknown or unexpected error occured.

    REVISIONS:
    Version 1.0  -- Nov 07, 1991
    Version 1.0a -- Nov 18, 1991
    Version 1.0c -- Jul 10, 1992
    Version 1.0f -- Aug 23, 1992
*/

#include <stdio.h>
#include <sys/types.h>
#include <sys/socket.h>
#include <netinet/in.h>
#include <arpa/inet.h>
#include <netdb.h>
#include <ctype.h>
#include <signal.h>
#include <errno.h>

#define DEFAULTTIMEOUT 20    /* in seconds */
#define SERVICEPORT "time"   /* name of port */
#define DEFAULTPORT 37       /* TIME/TCP port # */

#define DEBUG 0x1
#define VERBOSE 0x2
```

Listing 4.1   *continued*

```
int totsecs=1;       /* Time elapsed so far */
int timeout;         /* Time allowed to elapse */
int sckt;
char *hostname;      /* name of the remote host */
char opts;

extern int errno;    /*  */

void noconnect();
void noresponse();

main(argc,argv)
    char *argv[];
    int argc;
{
   struct hostent *host;
   struct servent *service;
   struct protoent *protocol;
   struct sockaddr_in pinghost,frompinghost;
   struct sockaddr_in localhost;
   int fromlen,res;
   long ipaddress;
   char buf[25];

   if((argc>1)&&(*argv[1]=='-'))
   {
      int offset=1;

      while(*(argv[1]+offset))
         switch(*(argv[1]+offset))
         {
          case 'd':         /* debug mode */
            opts|=DEBUG; offset++;
            break;
          case 'v':         /* verbose mode */
            opts|=VERBOSE; offset++;
            break;
          case NULL:        /* end of options list */
            break;
          default:          /* unknown option */
            offset++; break;
         }
   }
```

Listing 4.1 *continued*

```
   if(argc>1)
   {
      if(isdigit(*(argv[argc-1])))
      {
         if(strchr(argv[argc-1],'.'))
            hostname=argv[argc-1];
         else
            hostname=(argc-2) ? argv[argc-2] :
               argv[argc-1];
      }
      else
         hostname=argv[argc-1];
   }
   else
   {
      hostname=(char *)strrchr(argv[0],'/');
      if(hostname)
      {
         hostname++; *hostname=NULL;
      }
      else
         hostname = argv[0];
      fprintf(stderr, "Usage: %s -[dv] host [timeout]\n", hostname);
      exit(0);
   }

   if(isdigit(*(argv[argc-1])))
      timeout=atoi(argv[argc-1]); /* Define timeout */
   else
      timeout=DEFAULTTIMEOUT;     /* or default */

   /* Assume an IP address was given */

   if((ipaddress=inet_addr(hostname))==-1)
   {
      if(host=gethostbyname(hostname))
      {
         /* Found host, initialize the address */
         pinghost.sin_family=host->h_addrtype;
         bcopy(host->h_addr, (char *)&pinghost.sin_addr, host->h_length);
      }
```

Listing 4.1 *continued*

```
        else            /* UNKNOWN HOST */
        {
           /* Host unknown -- assume it is down */
           printf("%s: unknown host %s\n", argv[0],hostname);
           exit(1);
        }
    }
    else
    {
       pinghost.sin_addr.s_addr=ipaddress;
       pinghost.sin_family=AF_INET;
    }

    if(opts&DEBUG)
       printf("The IP Address for %s is: %01X\n", hostname,pinghost.sin_addr.s_addr);

    /* Define the activity port */
    /* I tried using getservbyname(), but it seemed to
       crash the program. I don't know why. */

    pinghost.sin_port=DEFAULTPORT;

    if(opts&DEBUG)
       printf("Service %s recognized as port # %d.\n", SERVICEPORT,pinghost.sin_port);

    /* Find the protocol by name (TCP/IP) */
    if(!(protocol=getprotobyname("tcp")))
    {
       printf("Unrecognized protocol: tcp\n");
       exit(255);
    }

    /* Make the socket on the local machine */
    if((sckt=socket(AF_INET,SOCK_STREAM,0))<0)
    {
       perror("socket"); exit(255);
    }

    if(opts&DEBUG)
       printf("Socket open. Descriptor Number %d\n", sckt);

    /* Set the alarm clock to go off in a second */

    signal(SIGALRM,noconnect); alarm(1);
```

Listing 4.1 *continued*

```c
/* Attempt the connection with remote machine. The
   EINTR is added so that when the alarm goes off and
   interrupts the system call, the call will recover. */

while(res=connect(sckt, (struct sockaddr *)&pinghost, sizeof(pinghost)))
{
   if(res==-1)                       /* error occured! */
   {
      if((opts&DEBUG)&&(errno!=EINTR))
         perror("connect");

      switch(errno)
      {
       case ECONNRESET:    /* reset connection */
       case ECONNREFUSED:  /* Connection refused */
         perror("connect");
         mypingexit(3);
         break;            /*  Exit CODE 3 */

       case EHOSTUNREACH:  /* Host is unreachable */
         perror("connect");
         mypingexit(5);
         break;            /*  Exit CODE 5 */

       case EINTR:         /* call interrupted */
       case EISCONN:       /* Connection exists */
         /* The connection was interrupted by alarm
            clock going off. The only way I know to
            reset the situation is to open a socket,
            and reattempt a connect() call */
         close(sckt);
         if((sckt=socket(AF_INET,SOCK_STREAM,0))<0)
         {
            perror("socket"); mypingexit(255);
         }
         break;
       case ENETRESET:     /* Dropped connection */
       case ENETDOWN:      /* Network down */
       case ENETUNREACH:   /* Network unreachable */
         perror("connect");
         mypingexit(4);
         break;            /*  Exit CODE 4 */
```

Listing 4.1 *continued*

```
      case EADDRINUSE:    /* Address in use */
      case EADDRNOTAVAIL: /* Address not available */
         break;           /* Ignore these. */

      default:            /* Unknown or unexpected */
         perror("connect");
         mypingexit(255);
         break;           /* Exit CODE 255 */
      }
   }

   if((opts&DEBUG)||(opts&VERBOSE))
      printf("Connect made (returned with %d)\n",res);

   /* Reset the alarm to call noresponse() when it xpires */
   signal(SIGALRM,noresponse); alarm(1);

   /* Just because the connect() succeeded, the machine may
      still be down. This portion tests the down-nessof the
      machine by waiting for a response from the connection. */

   while((res=recv(sckt,buf,sizeof(buf),0))<=0)
      if(res==-1)
      {
         if(opts&DEBUG)
         {
            perror("recv"); continue;
         }

         switch(errno)
         {
          case ECONNABORTED: /* connection aborted */
          case ENOTCONN:     /* no connection */
            perror("recv");  /* Exit CODE 1 */
            mypingexit(1);
            break;

          case ECONNRESET:   /* reset connection */
          case ENETRESET:    /* network reset */
            perror("recv");  /* Exit CODE 4 */
            mypingexit(4);
            break;

          default:           /* Unknown or unexpected */
            perror("recv");  /* Exit CODE 255 */
            mypingexit(255);
            break;
         }
      }
```

Listing 4.1 *continued*

```
        if((opts&DEBUG)||(opts&VERBOSE))
        {
            printf("Received something. ");
            printf("Len=%d. Total Elapsed Time: %d\n", res,totsecs);
        }

        /* Ignore any signals, they are meaningless now! */
        signal(SIGALRM,SIG_IGN);

        /* It's alive!! Let the user know */
        printf("%s is alive (%d)\n", hostname,totsecs);
        close(sckt);

        /* Pack it up, and take it home! */
        mypingexit(0);
    }
}
mypingexit(retcode)
      int retcode;
{
   close(sckt);
   exit(retcode);
}
/* End of File */
```

Listing 4.2   noconnect.c

```c
void noconnect()
{
   alarm(1);    /* Hit the snooze button */
   totsecs++;   /* Keep count of time passed */

   if((opts&DEBUG)||(opts&VERBOSE))
      printf("No connection after %d seconds!\n", totsecs-1);

   if(totsecs>timeout)
   {
     printf("%s not acknowledging connect attempt.\n", hostname);
     mypingexit(1);              /* Exit CODE 1 */
   }
}

/* End of File */
```

Listing 4.3   noresponse.c

```c
void noresponse()
{
   alarm(1);    /* Hit the snooze button */
   totsecs++;   /* Keep count of time passed */

   if((opts&DEBUG)||(opts&VERBOSE))
      printf("No response after %d seconds!\n", totsecs-1);

   if(totsecs>timeout)
   {
      printf("Connected to %s, but no response.\n", hostname,hostname);
      mypingexit(2);             /* Exit CODE 2 */
   }
}

/* End of File */
```

Listing 4.4   newping.sh.

```sh
#! /bin/sh -
#
#   A simple sh script to "newping" a list of important hosts.
#
#   Output goes to /dev/console
#

IMPHOSTS = polyslo phoenix blackbird zeus
TIMEOUT = 20

for HOST in $IMPHOSTS
do
   newping $IMPHOSTS $TIMEOUT
   CODE = $?

   DATE = `date +"%m-%d-%y %H:%M"`

#
#   Determine the appropriate English response.
#

   case $CODE in
      0) PHRASE=""
         STATUS=""
      1) PHRASE="No connection in $TIMEOUT secs."
         STATUS="down";;
      2) PHRASE="No response in $TIMEOUT secs."
         STATUS="hung";;
      3) PHRASE="Connection refused. "
         STATUS="rebooting";;
      4) PHRASE="Network unreachable from `hostname`."
         STATUS="unknown";;
      5) PHRASE="Host unreachable from `hostname`."
         STATUS="unknown";;
      *) PHRASE="Internal error."
         STATUS="unknown";;
   esac

   if [ "$PHRASE" != "" ]
   then
       echo "$DATE:$SITE $PHRASE  - ($STATUS)" > /dev/console
   fi
done

# End of File #
```

Chapter 5

Internet Online Services: archie

Christopher Bush

Introduction

The Internet, begun two decades ago as an experimental network of research and government agencies but later expanded to include a significant number of commercial corporations, provides access to an almost staggering amount of data and a wide range of information services. In this article, I describe in detail one of these services, *archie*. I outline the functionality of *archie*, explain how to use it, and explore issues involved with getting and installing two popular *archie* client programs on your system.

If you're not already connected, read the sidebar "Getting Connected" to find out how to get your system or systems connected to the Internet at a level of service that's right for you. In a subsequent article, I will discuss another Internet service that is rapidly growing in popularity, *gopher*. For your reference, the sidebar "What's Out There?" summarizes some of the most popular services available to Internet users.

Getting Connected

There are a number of ways to gain access to the Internet, each with its benefits and drawbacks. Ultimately, the type of connection you choose depends largely on what you and your company wish to achieve. If all you need is to exchange e-mail with other Internet users and you are operating on a tight budget, you may be satisfied with some form of dial-up access. On the other hand, if you want access to the full spectrum of services available to members of the Internet community, a dedicated connection is certainly the way to go. The following information describes some of the available methods of connection, approximate associated costs, necessary hardware and software, and various advantages and disadvantages worthy of consideration.

The cost information provided here is approximate and based on information obtained from the providers listed at the end of this sidebar.. It does not include telephone company charges, or charges for leased lines. Startup costs do not include any hardware or software which you may need to purchase to become "Internet ready." Services offered by each provider vary widely. You should check with each provider to find the service that's right for you.

What Is archie?

Information, including free software, on the Internet exists primarily in the form of publicly accessible files made available through the use of anonymous *ftp*. Anonymous *ftp* allows access to files on particular systems without requiring logins or passwords. Finding out which sites offer anonymous *ftp* and what

Dial Up

With dial-up access, your computer does not typically get its own Internet address. Instead, you are buying access on a computer operated by the service provider, and you gain access to the Internet from there. You simply connect to that computer using your modem, log in, and you're all set. Rates are reasonable, and usually are based on flat fee. There may also be fees based on connect time. You'll want a high-speed modem, at least 9600 baud. Great for home users whose needs are limited.
Fees:
Startup (one time): $0-$19
Recurring (monthly): $9-$45
Connect Time (hourly): $2.00-$8.50

SLIP/PPP

SLIP (Serial Line Internet Protocol) and *PPP* (Point to Point Protocol) services will bring you all the resources the Internet has to offer. Using normal voice quality phone lines, and a high-speed modem (V.32 or V.32bis), your computer (or every computer on your LAN) can have its own Internet address and access to the Internet through the system to which the modem is connected. This type of connection is usually offered on a demand (as needed) basis, where your modem dials the nearest connection point, or on a dedicated basis, where you use a leased line that is always connected. *SLIP* or *PPP* software will

files and software might be downloaded from them is where *archie* comes in.

archie is a means of maintaining and searching indexes of the files available from anonymous *ftp* sites on the Internet. These indexes of files are maintained on designated sites on the Internet, called *archie* servers. Numerous sites on the Internet operate as official *archie* servers, each containing the same information. Figure 5.1 lists these sites.

be required for your host computer. Versions of these software packages are available for many UNIX systems in the public domain. Service providers may provide you with this software, or help you find it. Not recommended for high traffic or interactive use. If your primary needs are for e-mail, USENET news, and FTP in low volume, this is a good, fairly low-cost solution.
Fees:
Startup (one time): $300-$1500
Recurring (monthly): $175-$275

Dedicated (Leased) Line

Line speeds typically are 56kbs (kilobits per second) and T1 (approximately 1.5Mb per second), and are dedicated digital quality lines typically leased from the local phone company or from companies such as Sprint or MCI. This requires a more substantial investment in hardware, including a router and a curiously named device called a CSU/DSU. This type of connection also gives you access to all the Internet services, from every node on your local network. This is how you'll want to go if you expect heavy interactive use, such as telnet or *rlogin* sessions to remote locations. Note, though, that a 56kbs line can be a bit unfriendly to this type of activity when traffic gets heavy.
Fees
Startup (one time): $2,000-$5,000
Recurring (monthly):56kbs: $425-$1,800
T1: $1,025-$3,000

```
archie.rutgers.edu    128.6.18.15       (Rutgers University)
archie.sura.net       128.167.254.179   (SURAnet archie server)
archie.unl.edu        129.93.1.14       (University of Nebraska in Lincoln)
archie.ans.net        147.225.1.2       (ANS archie server)
archie.au             139.130.4.6       (Australian server)
archie.funet.fi       128.214.6.100     (European server in Finland)
archie.doc.ic.ac.uk   146.169.11.3      (UK/England server)
archie.cs.huji.ac.il  132.65.6.15       (Israel server)
archie.wide.ad.jp     133.4.3.6         (Japanese server)
archie.ncu.edu.tw     140.115.19.24     (Taiwanese server)
```

Figure 5.1   archie *servers.*

Service Providers

PSI, Inc.
Suite 1100
11800 Sunrise Valley Drive
Reston, VA 22091
Phone: 1-(800)-82-PSI-82
E-mail: *info@psi.com*

UUNET Technologies, Inc.
Suite 570
3110 Fairview Park Dr.
Falls Church, VA 22042
Phone: 1-800-4-UUNET-3
E-mail: *alternet-info@uunet.uu.net*

Advanced Network and Services (ANS),
1875 Campus Commons Dr., Suite 220
Reston, VA 22091
Phone: 1-800-456-8267
E-mail: *info@ans.com*

NETCOM On-Line Communications Services
4000 Moorpark Ave., Suite 200
San Jose, CA 95117
Phone: 1-800-501-8649
E-mail: *info@netcom.com*

The information provided by an *archie* server comes in two forms. First, there is a database of filenames collected from all registered anonymous *ftp* sites. This database is updated regularly, typically once a month. The second type of information, called the "whatis" database, contains additional data describing the subject or function of the files. This is useful when the filename you are searching for may bear no resemblance to its purpose, particularly if it's software.

What's Out There?

The following list gives you a small taste of the kinds of services available to Internet users. Each service occupies its own little niche in the vast web of information that is the Internet.

finger

A utility used to find information about the users of a particular computer. You can *finger* a user at a remote site using a command like:

```
finger ryan@some.computer
```

If there is a user named *ryan* on *some.computer*, you might see this:

```
Login name: dryan                In real life: Dan Ryan
Directory: /usr/users/ryan       Shell: /bin/csh
Last login Fri Dec 24 23:57 on console
Unread mail since Sat Dec 18 21:12:03 1993
No Plan.
```

whois

Another utility used to find information about Internet users, usually those involved with the government, or network service providers.

Without *archie*, finding what you are looking for would be worse than thumbing through every page of a book, frantically searching for references to a particular topic. With it, a whole world of knowledge and software is merely an *ftp* session away.

Using archie

You can retrieve information from an *archie* server through one of several interfaces. The simplest interface requires only that you

E-mail

Perhaps the most frequently used service on the whole Internet. Whether it's with your brother-in-law at a university half-way across the country or another systems administrator on the other side of the globe, e-mail is a terrific way to exchange information.

Mailing Lists

Mail distribution lists that cater to various special interests. Mail sent to such a list is forwarded to each "subscriber," either a message at a time, or encapsulated in a digest form.

Anonymous ftp

Utility that makes files available to anyone on the Internet, without requiring a login and password on the computer acting as the anonymous *ftp* server. Users establish an *ftp* connection, log in as user anonymous, and, as a courtesy, send their e-mail address as a password. They then have the ability to get any file that has been made publicly available from that *ftp* server.

USENET News

Newsgroup, newsgroups, and more newsgroups — perhaps more aptly titled discussion groups. USENET (often called net news)

have the capability of sending and receiving electronic mail to one of the *archie* servers. You send an e-mail message to username *archie* at the server, issuing an *archie* command in the text of your message. The results of your command will be mailed back to you.

Once you have found what you are looking for, you must find a way to access it. Many anonymous *ftp* sites offer access via e-mail for users who cannot use *ftp* to connect directly to that site. This is usually accomplished by sending mail to user name

allows people to engage in on-line "conversations" with others having similar interests. Discussion groups cover a large number of topics grouped under general headings. Users "subscribe" to those groups of interest to them. Access to news is through the use of news reader software. Several news readers are available in the public domain. News groups of interest include *comp.sys.sgi.admin* and *comp.sys.sun.admin* for discussions related to administration of several popular UNIX systems.

archie

A useful way to find software and other files available from anonymous *ftp* sites. Information provided includes the path to the files and the name of the anonymous *ftp* server upon which they reside.

gopher

A menu-driven distributed client/server information system. *gopher* was developed at the University of Minnesota (The Gopher State), and is rapidly becoming one of the most widely used Internet resources. Using *gopher*, I can do everything from getting a local weather report to searching the card catalogs of the local university library without having to know that the information I retrieved came from two different computers in different locations.

ftpmail at the desired anonymous *ftp* site. Commands to *ftpmail* closely resemble those of "normal" *ftp*, and are entered in the text of your mail message.

If you have the ability to use telnet to connect to other sites on the Internet, you may choose the telnet interface to establish a connection to an *archie* server, as in the following example:

```
[2111:~ ]xanadu% telnet archie.rutgers.edu
```

To try a public access *gopher*: use telnet to connect to *consultant.micro.umn.edu*, and login with a user name of *gopher*.

WAIS (Wide Area Information Server)

A distributed client/server-based information system. WAIS servers contain indexes to the documents they make available. Using a WAIS client program, you can query those indexes until you find a reference to a desired topic. You can then use WAIS to look at each document. To get a sample of what you can do with WAIS, telnet to *quake.think.com*, login with user name WAIS.

World Wide Web

On the surface, World Wide Web (WWW) may appear much like *gopher*, and in fact you can access *gopher* servers equally well. The biggest distinction between the two is WWW's support of hypertext. Rather than being limited to the menu structure of *gopher*, you can follow hypertext links around the Web, searching for items of interest, and expanding upon topics as need arises. Its hypertext capability and integration with other services (*gopher* and WAIS) make the World Wide Web a powerful tool for information search and retrieval on the Internet.

When prompted for a login name, enter *archie*. You will not be asked for a password, and will soon see the *archie* server prompt:

archie>

At this point the *archie* server is ready to take your commands. Figure 5.2 shows a summary of the commands available using the telnet interface. Most of these are also available using the e-mail interface. A sample *archie* telnet session appears in Figure 5.3. In this example, a telnet connection is established with the *archie* server at Rutgers University. The *maxhits* variable is set to a value of 4, to limit the search result to a maximum of four entries. The search command, *prog*, is then used to search for file names containing the substring "*xarchie*." What is returned are entries for *ftp* servers matching this search, along with the pathnames of all files matching the search. From the abbreviated output given in the figure, you can see that two sites contain what appear to be compressed *tar* files of the *xarchie* software. One site has v2.02 of *xarchie*, the other has v1.3. Once you have a list of potential locations for the files you want, you can just fire up *ftp* and go get them.

```
bye      - same as "quit"
exit     - same as "quit"
help     - this message
list     - list the sites in the archie database
mail     - mail output to a user
nopager  - *** use 'unset pager' instead
pager    - *** use 'set pager' instead
prog     - search the database for a file
quit     - exit archie
set      - set a variable
show     - display the value of a variable
site     - list the files at an archive site
term     - *** use 'set term ...' instead
unset    - unset a variable
whatis   - search for keyword in the software description database
```

Figure 5.2   archie *commands.*

archie *Client Programs*

archie client programs connect to *archie* servers using a special protocol known as Prospero. These clients allow you to query an

```
[2112:~ ]xanadu% telnet archie.rutgers.edu
Trying 128.6.18.15 ...
Connected to dorm.Rutgers.EDU.
Escape character is '^]'.

SunOS UNIX (dorm.rutgers.edu) (ttyr2)

login: archie
Last login: Fri Oct 15 14:18:37 from bradley.che.utex
SunOS Release 4.1.3 (TDSERVER-SUN4C) #2: Mon Jul 19 18:37:02 EDT 1993

# Bunyip Information Systems, 1993

# Terminal type set to 'vt100 24 80'.
# 'erase' character is '^?'.
# 'search' (type string) has the value 'sub'.
archie> set maxhits 4
archie> prog xarchie
# Search type: sub.
# Your queue position: 3
# Estimated time for completion: 00:20
working... \

Host cs.columbia.edu    (128.59.16.20)
Last updated 00:39  3 Oct 1993

    Location: /archives/mirror3/linux/X11/xapps/comm
      FILE    -rw-rw-r--      369 bytes  02:13  7 May 1993  xarchie-2.0.2.README
      FILE    -rw-rw-r--   120725 bytes  02:13  7 May 1993  xarchie-2.0.2.tar.z

.
.
.

Host ftp.iastate.edu    (129.186.150.150)
Last updated 22:21  2 Oct 1993

    Location: /pub/386bsd/0.1-ports/utils/archie/xarchie-1.3
      FILE    -r--r--r--   179119 bytes  01:00  14 Feb 1993  xarchie-1.3.tar.Z
```

Figure 5.3   *Sample* archie *telnet session.*

archie server without having to connect to it with telnet and log in. This is typically the preferred method of accessing *archie* databases, as it places less of a burden on the computers which act as *archie* servers.

There are two primary *archie* client programs, *archie* and *xarchie*. The former is a command-line *archie* client, with *archie* commands passed as arguments to the command. The latter, *xarchie*, is an X Window application, providing a graphical user interface to *archie*. Both are available via anonymous *ftp* from several locations on the Internet.

Using the telnet interface, I found several sources for *archie* and *xarchie*. I used the anonymous *ftp* server *ftp.cs.widener.edu* to get *archie* v1.4.1 and *xarchie* v1.3 (there's a more recent version of *xarchie*, v2.0, which uses the X11 R5 libraries; but, since this version of the X Window system is perhaps not as widespread as X11 R4, I elected to use the earlier version of *xarchie*). Both clients were in the form of a compressed *tar* file.

Having acquired the two files with *ftp*, I set about installing them on my Sun workstation. Each package consists of the source code, makefiles, and various other support files to assist in compiling and installing the software. On my Sun workstation, running SunOS v4.1.3, I was able to build the command-line *archie* client with no modifications to the makefile. You should check the value of the *ARCHIE* variable in the makefile, and make sure it is set to an appropriate *archie* server (the available servers are listed in the makefile). Give some thought to this, as this will be the default server that the *archie* client will connect to (it's a good idea to pick one that is geographically close to you). After editing the makefile, simply run the make command. If all goes well, you will have an executable file called *archie* which you should then copy to a common directory found in your users' *PATH* variable — perhaps */usr/local/bin* or something similar. You can then copy a "man page," *archie.man*, to a common location on your system for online reference pages. That's it, you have an *archie* client.

Those of you with X Window-based workstations or terminals will probably prefer the *xarchie* client. Compiling this gets a little more complicated than the command-line client, but is still straightforward. The software includes a file, called *README*, with detailed instructions for getting *xarchie* up and running on your system. If you are familiar with *Imake* and *Imakefiles*, you'll have no problem.

The *xarchie* client has an intuitive graphical interface, making *archie* queries much easier. Buttons and pull-down menus across the top of the window give access to the settings and commands. Three scrolling lists give the server names, directory names, and file names returned by the *archie* server as a result of your query. Simply enter your search term in the text field in the lower portion of the window, click on the Query button at the top, and after (usually) a short wait, the results of your query will display. Using your mouse and the scroll bars, search through the list of results. If you find what you are looking for, you may be able to get the file automatically by clicking on the *ftp* button at the top of the window.

Both *archie* clients are easy to use, and definitely to be preferred over interactive telnet sessions by *archie* servers. Neither client offers a way to query the "whatis" database, however. I prefer the graphical user interface of *xarchie*; if you're a little more adventurous, go out and find *xarchie* v2.0.2, the interface is much nicer than v1.3.

Conclusion

archie has become an invaluable addition to my systems administration "toolbox." Using the *xarchie* client, I am able to find and retrieve software and documents that I would otherwise not even know about. As an example, I recently stumbled across a number of documents relating to Solaris v2.2, the latest offering from Sun Microsystems in the UNIX SVR4 arena. These documents proved to be worth their transfer time in gold, as I had just struggled for several days with many of the features of Solaris which they dealt with. I have used *xarchie* to locate a number of software packages that have become permanent additions to the computer systems I manage, including the Perl programming language, the GNU project's compilers and other development tools, the COPS security software, and more. All of these are freely available, if only you know where to look.

archie can do a lot for you, even in the narrow scope of information it covers. To really exploit the power of the Internet, you'll want to explore some of the other services. In a subsequent article, I'll discuss *gopher* in detail, including how you can use gopher to provide information to the users of your systems.

Recommended Reading

Krol, Ed. *The Whole INTERNET User's Guide & Catalog.* Sebastopol, CA: O'Reilly & Associates, Inc., 1992. ISBN 1-56592-025-2

Chapter 6

Internet Online Services: gopher

Christopher Bush

Introduction

In the last chapter, I introduced you to *archie*, a simple yet powerful tool for retrieving information from the Internet. One of *archie*'s shortcomings is its limited ability to perform topic-oriented searches. For the most part, when you look something up with *archie*, you are matching a search string against a file or directory name. When you are searching for a particular piece of software that is freely available, this doesn't usually present a problem. For instance, if I want to find the latest version of the *perl* programming language, I know that a reasonable thing to do with *archie* is use a search string of "perl." However, if I'm looking for a 1990 census report for Massena, New York, using *archie* only leads to a dead end. That doesn't mean I won't find that information somewhere on the Internet, nor does it necessarily mean that the information doesn't exist on an anonymous *ftp* site registered with the official *archie* servers. It only means that I will have difficulty locating the information using a keyword search like "massena." In fact, after several attempts, with several different search strings, I was unable to find what I was looking for with *archie*. So, how can I find this information on the Internet? I used *gopher*!

What Is gopher?

gopher is an Internet information search and retrieval system, developed by the Computer and Information Services department at the University of Minnesota. With *gopher* you can gain access to a wide variety of information both inside and outside your organization. *gopher* presents information to you in the form of menu screens. By selecting a menu item of interest, you may either be retrieving a text file, accessing another menu, or executing a telnet session to access a particular resource. The information

```
              Internet Gopher Information Client 2.0 p110

                           University of Minnesota

   -->  1.  Information About Gopher/
        2.  Computer Information/
        3.  Discussion Groups/
        4.  Fun & Games/
        5.  Internet file server (ftp) sites/
        6.  Libraries/
        7.  News/
        8.  Other Gopher and Information Servers/
        9.  Phone Books/
        10. Search Gopher Titles at the University of Minnesota <?>
        11. Search lots of places at the University of Minnesota  <?>
        12. University of Minnesota Campus Information/

   Press ? for Help, q to Quit, u to go up a menu              Page: 1/1
```

Figure 6.1   *University of Minnesota* gopher.

that a particular menu choice leads you to may come from the local system or network, or it may be a link to another *gopher* server on a computer on the other side of the world.

Figure 6.1 shows the main menu of the *gopher* server running at the University of Minnesota. Using *gopher* is as simple as choosing the item from the current menu that seems to be most relevant, and continuing until you find what you want. If at any time you find you've strayed away from your intended goal, you can retreat to the previous menu.

Like *archie*, *gopher* consists of server software for providing the information, and client software for accessing the information. In this article, I discuss both sides of *gopher*. Two primary *gopher* clients are available from the University of Minnesota, one for ASCII terminal users and one for X Window capable systems. I will briefly cover the *gopher* server, and what types of information you can present with it.

I recommend that you begin by downloading the *gopher* software. The best place to go is right to the source, the University of Minnesota. Using anonymous *ftp*, connect to *boombox.micro.umn.edu*. Enter "anonymous" as a username, and your e-mail address as a password. Once you're in, change to directory */pub/gopher/UNIX*. Here you will find a number of compressed *tar* files for the *gopher* software. You'll want to retrieve *gopher2.010.tar.Z*; if you have X Window capabilities on your network, get *xgopher.1.3.2.tar.Z* as well (in both cases the version number may be higher by the time you read this). The first file contains the software for both the *gopher* server, and the *gopher* client for ASCII terminals. The second file is the X Window System-based client. You'll also want to retrieve the "Gopher Guide" from */pub/gopher/docs*. This document is available either as a PostScript file or as straight text. Remember to put *ftp* into binary mode before transferring the files.

gopher *Client Programs*

The ASCII terminal client, *gopher*, is part of the *gopher* distribution file, *gopher2.010.tar.Z*, which also contains the *gopher* server software. The X Window-based client is in *xgopher1.3.2.tar.Z*.

When you extract the main *gopher* distribution, the directory that is created will contain a *makefile* at the top level that builds both the client and server software. Before you try building the software, read the file *INSTALL*, located in the *doc* subdirectory, for detailed information on getting started. You'll need to edit two files to get *gopher* compiled and installed properly, *Makefile.config* and *conf.h*. Both are located at the top level of the *gopher* directory, and both contain explicit instructions for changing the values of various variables so as to customize *gopher* for your environment.

Perhaps the most important settings are in *conf.h*. These are *CLIENT1_HOST*, *CLIENT2_HOST*, *CLIENT1_PORT*, and *CLIENT2_PORT*. The first two relate to the default hosts that the *gopher* client will attempt to connect to. If you intend to run your own *gopher* server or servers, set these to the host names of the primary and secondary *gopher* servers you want for defaults. The latter two variables tell the *gopher* client which TCP port number to use when attempting to connect to the *gopher* server. The default of 70 is appropriate unless that port is already in use on the computer where your *gopher* server will be running. If that is the case you'll need to change the default to the number of an unused port.

Makefile.config contains variables related to what compiler you will use on your system, and the names of the directories where you would like the various pieces of the *gopher* software to be installed. Once you have made all the necessary changes, you can build the software by executing *make*. If you only want to build the client software, use

```
% make client
```

Once you've successfully built the client software, you can run it. If you didn't change the default host, *gopher* will connect to the predefined default, which is the *gopher* server at the University of Minnesota. This will display the menu shown in Figure 6.1.

Once you are confident that your *gopher* client is built properly, you can install it, providing you made the appropriate changes to *Makefile.config*, by typing

```
% (cd gopher; make install)
```

The other important piece of client software is *xgopher*. This program provides a simple graphical user interface, where menu items can be selected via mouse, and files are displayed in a separate window. If a *gopher* server is making graphics image files available, selecting them causes *gopher* to bring them up using the viewer you have specified in the configuration file. This functionality requires a program like *xv* or *xloadimage*, both readily available from numerous anonymous *ftp* sites (*archie*, described in the previous issue, would be a good way to find these). The *xgopher* client, like the *xarchie* client, uses an *imakefile*, and is simple to build (read the *README* file before you begin). There is also a *conf.h* file to be modified, as in the ASCII client. Again, an important element in this file is the name of the default *gopher* server to which *xgopher* will connect.

The gopher *Server*

If, after some experience with *gopher* or *xgopher*, you decide that the users on your network could benefit from a local *gopher* server, you'll need to compile the *gopher* server software. After modifying *Makefile.config* and *conf.h*, as discussed above, you can build the server software by typing

```
% make server
```

To install the *gopher* server, execute

```
% (cd gopherd; make install)
```

This will install the *gopher* server, *gopherd*, and its supporting files in the locations you named during configuration. You'll then need to set up the host on which *gopherd* will run, to ensure that the *gopher* server will be run whenever the computer is rebooted. You can do this using start-up scripts like */etc/rc.local*, or you can add an entry to the *inetd.conf* file, if your system uses *inetd*. You'll want to read Chapter 7 of the *Gopher Guide*, "Configuring the UNIX Server," which has detailed information on this setup.

There's more to be done than just getting the *gopher* server running on your network. You must also decide what kinds of information you will make available. Figure 6.2 lists the types of information that *gopher* can present to your users. One of the options you set in *Makefile.config* is the location of your *gopher* data. This location will initially be a directory which you create. The contents of this directory determine how your information will be presented to *gopher* clients connecting to your server. The contents of the top-level *gopher* directory represent the first menu that a *gopher* client user will see. If there are subdirectories, choosing those brings you to another menu, whose entries will be the contents of that subdirectory. Ordinary text files will be displayed to the user upon selection. Files whose names begin

```
0 - Text File
1 - Directory
2 - CSO name server
4 - Mac HQX file
7 - Full Text Index
8 - Telnet session
9 - Binary file
s - sound file
I - image file
```

Figure 6.2   gopher *document types.*

with a period are special files, called links, which I'll discuss in detail later. Other defaults for files within your *gopher* data directory relate to sound files, graphics images (GIF), and other types. The "Gopher Guide" details all of these.

Where *gopher* gets interesting is with the links, or "dot files." These files, which will not show up directly on the *gopher* menu, can be used to refer to *gopher* data on your own system, or from other *gopher* servers on the Internet. Figure 6.3 shows an example of one of these links. The *Numb* field is used to place a menu item at a specific position in the *gopher* menu. The *Name* field is used to specify the text that will appear in the *gopher* menu for that item. The *Type* field corresponds to the type of the *gopher* data, as presented in Figure 6.2. *Port* represents the TCP port number of the *gopher* server being linked to. Path specifies the path within the *gopher* data directory of the server where the information is located. *Host* is the fully qualified domain name of the host where the *gopher* server is running. The example in Figure 6.3 is a link to a *gopher* directory at *gopher.internet.com*. The title of the entry, as it would appear on your *gopher* client session is "Internet World Magazine." One important point to note here is that the *gopher* server in this case is being run on TCP port 2100, rather than the default port 70.

As you explore the Internet using *gopher*, you will come across information of interest to your users. Rather than rely on their finding such things themselves, you may choose to create links

```
#
Type=1
Name=Internet World Magazine
Path=1/collected/internet_world
Host=gopher.internet.com
Port=2100
URL: gopher://gopher.internet.com:2100/11/collected/internet_world
```

Figure 6.3 gopher *link example.*

to them somewhere within your own *gopher* data directory. Both *gopher* clients mentioned in this article can tell you how to create your own link. From the *gopher* ASCII client, position the menu pointer on an item of interest and press the = key. This will present you with a screen containing the values of the various fields used in a link. From *xgopher*, clicking the mouse on the "Info about selection" button accomplishes the same thing. Once you have this information, you are ready to create your own link. Create a file with a name beginning with a period in your *gopher* data directory. Enter the appropriate information for each field described in the preceding paragraph. You need not restart the *gopherd* process to "see" the new data. The next time a *gopher* client connects, the new information will be available. You may also want to create the link shown in Figure 6.4. This will take you to a menu listing all of the "known" *gopher* servers in the world (that is, all those who have registered with the maintainers of this information at the University of Minnesota). This link provides a useful starting point for exploring gopherspace.

veronica

veronica (Very Easy Rodent-Oriented Net-wide Index to Computerized Archives) is a service by which you can perform keyword searches on the titles available in gopherspace. *veronica* searches are launched from your *gopher* client, and the results are presented to you as another *gopher* menu, from which you can

```
Type=1
Name=All gopher servers in the world
Path=1/Other Gopher and Information Servers/all
Host=gopher2.tc.umn.edu
Port=70
URL: gopher://gopher2.tc.umn.edu:70/11/Other Gopher and Information Servers/all
```

Figure 6.4   *List of all knwon* gophers.

select any of the items returned as a result of the search. Figure 6.5 gives the link information you can use in your *gopher* server to enable your users to make *veronica* searches.

Conclusion

I have only scratched the surface of the features and functionality of *gopher*. For complete and definitive information, check out the *Gopher Guide*.

gopher provides tremendous potential as an information system in a networked environment. You can use it either as a "bulletin board" on your own local network or as a means of providing information to the Internet at large. Give *gopher* a try. Use it to explore the Internet for a while. You'll be amazed at what you can find in gopherspace.

Recommended Reading

Krol, Ed. *The Whole INTERNET User's Guide & Catalog.* Sebastopol, CA: O'Reilly & Associates, 1992. ISBN 1-56592-025-2.

```
#
Type=1
Name=Search gopherspace using Veronica
Path=1/veronica
Host=futique.scs.unr.edu
Port=70
URL: gopher://futique.scs.unr.edu:70/11/veronica
```

Figure 6.5   veronica *search link.*